A BOOK OF

Wisdom

FOR

Angels

_____

by Donald Piranty

_____

Illustrations by **Susan Tower**
Sacred Site Art, Soul Paintings,
Animal Totem Paintings and Pet Portraits

Graphic Design by Susan Tower
www.SusanTower.com
susantower1@gmail.com

———————————

Edited by **Livea Cherish**

———————————

Published by **Practical Holistic Living Network**
Hot Springs, Arkansas
Brenda McDaniel R.N., C.H.T.
thereikimaster@gmail.com

www.PracticalHolisticLiving.com

*Our Goal is to provide tools, contacts, education,
and information to help the average person
find practical ways of living and demonstrating
holistic life styles beneficial to themselves,
their families and the planet.*

Preface

The wisdom in this book was channeled in the light of love for all the Angels currently incarnated on this planet, and I choose to see it as a gift to those who are struggling to stay on their life path here on Earth. I dedicate these pages to my own personal angel who is always by my side, in good times and bad, regardless of whether I choose to acknowledge her or not.

There are so many times when my mental and physical reality become so overpowering that I just want to sink into the oblivion of it all; it is exactly at these most precious of moments that I feel her by my side, and she whispers some magical words to bring me back to the belief, trust and reality of my own True Life-Path.

Out there in the world, it seems that there are so few of us – yet I know that there are so many. Many of us feel lost and displaced by the challenges and rigors of this reality.

Yet if we are to achieve our goals then we must go on. I sincerely hope that this small token will make a difference to some of you. If only one is kept on or returned to their path, then that will be enough.

With grateful thanks to all those involved in bringing this work into physical reality.

Love and Light Always,

Donald Piranty

Introduction

It has been over eight years since I was awakened in the middle of the night from the deepest of sleep with a voice repeatedly nagging in my head the words, "To fail is a terrible thing, but the real tragedy is when we give up trying." Wow! That's good, I need to write that down... but I'm so tired. I can say that I was going through a particularly bad time in my life and relationship, everything up in the air and nothing working out, but all I had on my mind that night on going to bed was the fact I was very tired and badly wanted a good night's sleep.

It's not unusual that I receive information at night in the form of words or dreams. Many of you are probably aware of the difficulty in waking up enough so that you can accurately record the event... and of course there is never a pen when you need it.

That was one of those nights...

Ok, I give in. I'll get up and write it down if only to shut you up. I noticed it was around 3:00 am; I went to the kitchen, found paper and pen, got it down and with a sigh of relief went back to bed. Now leave me alone and let me sleep.

I had barely closed my eyes again when another verse started to come through. And of course I had left the pen and paper in the kitchen, so back up again and write it down; surely that was the last of it.

Back to bed. But the nagging just went on and on, one after the other. Well, to cut a long story short, around 40 verses and three and a half hours later, it stopped. And bless them, I was then too tired to go back to sleep.

It took me several days to realize what I had been given, and in the interceding years the "Angel Book" has been a source of comfort and inspiration for me and my friends. I like to use it when I have a worry or problem and just open it to a random page – surprising how that works.

It's probably due to the fact that I have always felt the words were put into my hands and never really had anything to do with me, other than my being a catalyst for its manifestation. I never imagined it would actually 'go public'. For that I wish to thank Brenda McDaniel of Practical Holistic Living Network who obviously had more vision and faith than I. Angels manifest in the most mysterious of places... Thank you Brenda.

Donald Piranty 2011

I became aware
that I am an Angel.

Because of this
every one of
my expectations
is a positive one.

And to my
surprise and delight,
every
outcome
is so much better
than I ever Imagined!

10 Rules for Surviving as an Angel

1. Do not sacrifice yourself for anyone else. They would not want you to, and it's not appreciated anyway.

2. Even with the strength of a thousand angels, it is not possible to heal the sick, give wise counsel or make the sad happy... unless THEY choose to let you.

3. You are a natural catalyst for other people; of this, you must at all times be aware... and responsible.

4. Always put aside a portion of each day to remember your task. Connect to your heart and give thanks to your guides and helpers.

5. Understand that play and laughter are essential parts of your angel makeup. So, strive to laugh and play as much as possible, with as many people as you can.

6. Angels require music and nature to replenish their energies. So, commune with these things at least once a day.

7. Deep down, you will always have an incredibly strong "knowing" that you can fly. If you must attempt this in the physical, make sure you have a parachute or aeroplane!

8. With a smile and laughter, always do your best to bring out the "happy child" in all you meet.

9. As often as possible, make time to stop and watch a complete and glorious sunrise/sunset. For to partake in this is to commune with God.

10. And finally... Do not take yourself or your job too seriously; after all, in the end... it's still an illusion.

Lying waiting, hidden in the darkness that
surrounds us,
is the perfect pure diamond of realization,
a gift from God to each of us.

We only have to light up our lives with joy, love
and happiness, and in that light the
perfect beauty of our diamond will be revealed.

Love is present and "offered" around
every corner of our lives...

Finding love is not the problem,
the knack is knowing what to do with it
once it's been offered.

Sometimes, in our very worst moments...
when we think we most need rescuing,

It is in that moment that we are best
able to rescue someone else.

Then to our amazement...
The rescuer becomes the rescued!

Those with strong minds create

new futures and realities.

Others

simply choose

which one to attach to.

The determination to succeed

must be greater than

the desire to

fail.

Life becomes tedious and boring

when we fall into a rut

and stop living!

You choose to be

whatever you continue to be –

a success, a failure, or an in-between.

To succeed

or attain anything

we desire

(good or bad),

we require only

the unconditional willingness

to do anything that is necessary.

The needs of the soul are infinitely greater

than those of the body.

It just feels like the other way around!

An unpleasant fact:

We can make ourselves sick

when we refuse to acknowledge

that our bodies need rest, attention or love!

It is just when we hit rock bottom
and really want to give up

That we should stop, take a breath
and make ourselves

see just how much positive
there is in our lives.

You are not alone...

You have Angels

who guide you

who protect you

who give you inspiration

and just plain love you.

Don't forget to occasionally say

thank you!

Consider this:

Ill heath is the consequence of unhappiness...

unhappiness is the consequence of ill health.

Believe that you are moving toward

a brighter future.

Don't hold yourself up by focusing

on things

you THINK you

might have done wrong.

If life has kicked and battered

you to the floor, you lie there dazed

and punch drunk, not knowing what to do,

or which way to turn...

It is never as bad as it feels at the time.

Believe it!

If you look inside you will be rewarded

with the truth.

Believe it!

You can get back up and start again.

this you MUST believe!

Every one of life's storms shakes your world

and creates the opportunity for change.

Universal law requires that all life

must move and change.

If you stand still and refuse this

you will surely start to stagnate and die.

If you are the only person in the world

who knows with absolute certainty

that you are an Angel,

Then hold onto that

with all your strength!

For they may deny you now,

but you will be surprised

how many believe in you

when they have nowhere else to turn.

Music is food for the soul…
Make EVERY day your MUSIC DAY!

There is music to stimulate
every mood.

Choose some now to enhance or change yours.

You never know –

YOU COULD FEEL LIKE DANCING!

Unhappy people are
seldom seen DANCING.

Believe in Yourself!

Your every action is a pebble

thrown in the pond of life.

Never underestimate

the power and effect

of your ripples.

Once an Angel

always an Angel.

There is no going back –

just the choice on whether

you accept that or deny it!

To every being who comes into your life:

Be open and welcoming

never judgmental.

The largest, brightest diamonds

are sometimes found

in the least likely of places.

Some of the greatest

incarnated Angels in history

never knew they were Angels at all!

There is no such thing

as a sad Angel...

only Angels who

choose

to look like they are!

Angels on earth are at the

cutting edge...

probably the most difficult

job in the universe!

Be proud of the body you inhabit

which enables you to do your work.

Keep it immaculate

as you would do with any gift from God.

When you are feeling lonely
or depressed

picture a happy moment

playing with young children

and your wings

will lift you again.

A wise Angel never worries about

where to go or

whom to work with...

These things are brought to you.

so stop worrying,

follow your intuition, trust,

and go with the flow!

If you become aware
that stillness surrounds you
like being in the eye of a storm

Don't fret.
Just enjoy it while it lasts.

Rest assured
your Angels are working
very hard behind the scenes.

TO FAIL

IS A TERRIBLE THING.

BUT

THE REAL TRAGEDY

IS WHEN WE GIVE UP TRYING!

The new flames

of an idea

can only grow...

if nurtured

by the strong

steady breath

of belief.

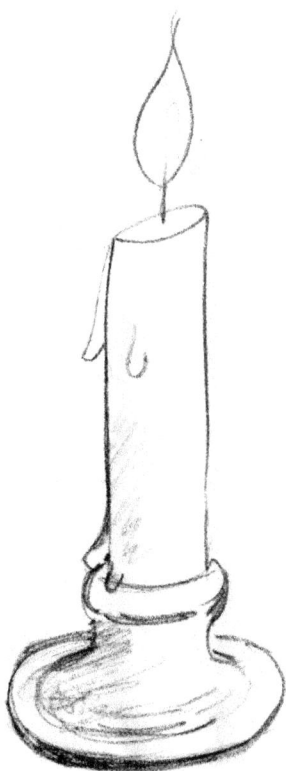

Everywhere we look

humankind

is pushing the envelope

of our reality.

Anything now seems possible.

Like children in a garden, will we now

nurture or destroy?

We harness ourselves

to the yoke of life

afraid to spread our wings

and experience the

freedom of living.

Surrendering
completely and absolutely
to another human being
in trust and love
is the greatest gift we can bestow...

Should two people
do this unconditionally for each other
then they will take on
each other's positive traits
and balance out the negative...

Working as an Angel speeds up our frequency.

The higher our frequency

the faster we manifest the things

we imagine and think about.

Trouble is, most of us spend so much more time

imagining and thinking negative things

than the positive.

Stop!

Sit down right now and draw a map

of where you want your life to go.

You'll feel much better!

Let's get one thing straight...

Most people are
scared and unhappy.

The way to keep your
frequency up

is to be fearless
and
very happy!

Your body is a

high frequency miracle.

To nurture it requires

quality not quantity.

Listen carefully

to what it is telling you!!

If you are procrastinating

thinking or worrying about doing something…

Then have no fear… let go!

It's not Angel work!

If you rely on others for your

success or happiness

then you will surely draw

the OPPOSITE to yourself!

We need to be content with

who and where we are

in this moment...

as well as focused on

solid goals for the future!

Doing "Angel work" can be

very lonely at times...

I wonder why it never feels that way!

Sometimes, my human experience is so dark,
light seems to cease to exist; I feel only the beat of
hate and pain. In the all-pervading darkness my heart
shrinks to nothing as the surge of sorrow from and
for the whole human race overwhelms me.

I feel I am drowning, choking on despair.
The blackness cloaks me, I feel lost forever...

And then...

I stand alone on the high cliff
in the emerging dawn,
watching the unfolding blaze of glory
as the new day emerges.

Inspired, in my mind's eye,
I hear the innocent laughter and see the
happiness, as children play.

I see a mother's face light up,
as she looks for the first time
at her newborn baby.

I wonder at the courage,
seeing a person saving the life of another.

But above all, I see,

even in the most

unlikely of places

unconditional

unreserved LOVE.

This is God

demonstrated in

humanity.

And my life fills

with light again.

Angels or Humans

REMEMBER

You all chose this reality –
this exact location,
these exact circumstances,
together with all the good and bad.

So next time you feel like

having a 'go' at someone...

have a laugh

at yourself instead.

Notes

Notes

Notes

Published by
Practical Holistic Living Network
Hot Springs, Arkansas

Look for our two upcoming books:

"Heart Shadows of a Wounded Healer"
by Brenda McDaniel

"The Crystal Devas"
by Brenda McDaniel

For more information, contact:
thereikimaster@gmail.com
www.PracticalHolisticLiving.com